THE

REVENGE

BY

LOVE

THE REVENGE BY LOVE

DAVID DOOLEY

STORY LINE PRESS
1995

Story Line Press
Three Oaks Farm
Brownsville, OR 97327

This publication was made possible thanks in part to the generous support of the Nicholas Roerich Museum, the Andrew W. Mellon Foundation, the National Endowment for the Arts, and our individual contributors.

Book design by Chiquita Babb

Library of Congress Cataloging-in-Publication Data
Dooley, David, 1947–
    The revenge by love / David Dooley.
      p. cm.
    ISBN 1-885266-06-5
    I. Title.
  PS3554.O567R4 1995
  811'.54—dc20   95-6895
                 CIP

Some of the poems in this book originally appeared in other publications. I would especially like to thank Frederick Morgan and the other editors of the *Hudson Review* for their loyal belief in my work.

    Beloit Poetry Journal: "Judith," "A Conversation," "Flowers"
    The Hudson Review: "Stieglitz Talking to the Disciples, 1916," "Stieglitz: Early Photographs of O'Keeffe," "Lake George," "Observations," "Stieglitz Aging" (as "Stieglitz, 1931-32"), "Lake George in Winter," "New Mexico," "Ghost Ranch," "The Waiter," "Zoramel"
    New Texas '91: "Dirt"

FOR ALLEN

TABLE OF CONTENTS

"A Curious Triumphant Feeling About Life":
The Poetry of David Dooley   ix

I

A Few Last Things   3
Zoramel   5
Politics   8
And Part of Her Anus in Dallas   11
The Waiter   14
Dirt   15
Camille in Luxor: Saint-Saens Visits Egypt, 1896   17
Sweet Youth   19
A Little Hunger   21
Lillian's Elegy   23
Sun Pictures   26

II
O'Keeffe and Stieglitz

Stieglitz Talking to the Disciples, 1916   33
Stieglitz: Early Photographs of O'Keeffe   35
Lake George   37
Judith   38
A Conversation   39
Flowers   40
Observations   43
Stieglitz Aging   44

Lake George in Winter   46
New Mexico   48
Ghost Ranch   51

Notes   55

"A CURIOUS TRIUMPHANT FEELING ABOUT LIFE": THE POETRY OF DAVID DOOLEY

David Dooley concluded his first collection, *The Volcano Inside*, with "Take Five," a dramatic monologue spoken by a movie director. Early in the poem, the narrator comments on a boat crucial to the scene being filmed:

> I know it's really a workboat,
> but say your line anyway, darling, half the audience
> will think it really is a houseboat, and the rest will think
> I'm a bloody genius for having you say it's a houseboat
> when it isn't.

That readiness selectively, and tellingly, to alter the facts to suit what Dante called the larger truth marks David Dooley's accomplishment as a poet; his willingness to tell us what he's doing even while he's doing it bespeaks the confidence of a magician who gives away the secret even as he performs the trick, certain we will be dazzled anyway. Even this poem's title, with references to slang, cinema, jazz, and the five characters involved, displays Dooley's characteristic layering of effect.

Donald Hall observed in a review of *The Volcano Inside*, "David Dooley uses justly observed speech to fix character. The rush of someone talking . . . constructs a firm reality of speaking character. . . . [His] poetry . . . is energetic, often long-lined and propulsive, with a headlong compelling rhythm." This speaks primarily to the surface quality of the poems, and Dooley's more recent poems, gathered in this new collection, demonstrate continued facility with heard voices and flexible long lines, though several of the poems in the second section, a sequence concerning the lives, marriage, and art of Georgia O'Keeffe and Alfred Stieglitz, evidence equal ease with shorter, more epigrammatic or haiku-like structures. Hall indicates as well, if briefly, the ends toward which Dooley applies his craft: the subtle ways he uses speech and situation to develop personality fully, allowing us to see all sides of a character while withholding judgment, and inviting us, as well, not to dismiss a character's strengths or the truth of his or her utterance just because we come to see that character's human flaws. In short, Dooley's best poems invite us to know these characters the way we know real people: in their fullness.

Readers familiar with Dooley's first collection will find in the first half of *The Revenge by Love* poems that develop and refine structures and subjects introduced in that book, particularly dramatic monologues like "Dirt" and "Politics," humorous explorations of characters drawn from decidedly different ends of the demographic spectrum. In the first, a West Texan regales his date with stories of a boyhood friend—a compulsively messy ne'er-do-well—that reveal, through strategies reminiscent of the best of Browning or Frost, more about the speaker than he suspects. "Politics," on the other hand, eavesdrops on the gay scion of an old-moneyed family discoursing—as veiled flirtation—on politics and homosexuality to a younger male auditor. In these, as other of Dooley's monologues, speaker, situation, and auditor are presented clearly and economically—"dramatic" in the fullest sense.

Consider how selection of detail and accurate presentation of idiom work to present a full but restrained emotional register in these lines from another of the dramatic monologues, "Lillian's Elegy":

> I wonder that Michael wasn't at the funeral,
> you don't suppose, no, I'm too tired to suppose.
> Too tired to do much except go lie down beside Daddy.
> The thought of that bed. Right before daylight,
> to see Paul's face come I-spying up over the crib.
> "Ooh," he'd say. "Ooh." I'd change and powder him
> and tuck him up against Daddy, then go down to warm the milk.
> Betty never woke up. Slept as hard as she did everything else.

Even this brief excerpt provides a full sense of character and situation: the son dead of AIDS, the addressed lover, the hint of resentment toward the surviving daughter. The language here, as in other of Dooley's poems, belies the care and precision of selection; masters of diction need not display a vast working vocabulary in every line. Yet each word rings true to the speaker's background. Even constructions like "I-spying," which I've never before heard used in this way, seem accurate, precise—all the more impressive if it is invented. And the rhythm, while reflecting speech, pushes conversation toward formal pattern, aided by the understated use of assonance and consonance. The associative structure, while reflecting the speaker's distracted state of mind, moves the reader through a controlled sequence of thoughts.

Notable, too, are the third-person poems, oblique monologues, that shift narrative distance seamlessly. In cinematic terms, Dooley demonstrates an ability to move from a long shot to a close-up, then back out, by means of diction. This technique is introduced early in the first poem, "A Few Last Things," which concerns an aging scholar reminiscing about matters trivial and profound, though the treatment suggests that, nearing the end of his days, even the central character is no longer sure of the distinction between these.

> He'd imagined leaving a testament,
> a parchment scroll bearing a secret doctrine
> to kindle the initiates, or a plain speech
> where "tree" would mean tree and "light" only light,
> or words steely with wisdom, polished epigrams
> reflecting a lifetime's understanding. Wrongheaded again.

The narrative stance in the first lines of this passage allows for exploration of the character's thoughts at some remove—"He'd imagined"—and holds us at a distance from these thoughts through elevated diction and revealing imagery: "parchment scroll," "kindle the initiates," "words steely with wisdom." These clichés reflect the character's pretensions, exposing how unoriginal he can be in imagining his own original contribution. Even his desire to use words to mean "only" what they mean is ironic; in this instance, these words would come to "mean" something about his skill with language. The simple phrase, "Wrongheaded again," drops the level of diction into the colloquial, and the use of a sentence fragment undercuts the accumulation of the long preceding sentence. This abrupt shift of diction and syntax also collapses narrative distance, moving us closer to the character's "real" thoughts.

The greatest departure—in both senses—is this volume's second section, the extended sequence "O'Keeffe and Stieglitz." The use of historical figures is new for Dooley, foreshadowed perhaps by "How I Wrote It," the opening poem of *The Volcano Inside*, whose speaker is loosely modeled on Henry Miller, but there Miller served as an archetype of the profane artist, allowing Dooley to explore the tension between surface crudity and a deep appreciation of beauty. This volume's "Camille in Luxor: Saint-Saens Visits

Egypt, 1896" marks Dooley's first real foray into this territory. Estranged from his wife, whom he holds responsible for the death of their infant son, the composer winters "remote from Parisian fogs," drawn by the strangeness but holding the experience at a comfortable distance:

> Mornings he was content to observe
> the half-hidden temple rising above the quay,
> or look across the river to villages built of mud, where
> buffaloes sank up to the shoulder dragging their yokes,
> or in the marketplace to be jostled by guides,
> beggars, donkey boys, Copts tattooed with crosses,
> a one-eyed vendor hawking morsels of roast mutton.
> Cacophonies of language, such strange perfumes.

Observing and looking, yet not quite intoxicated by the exotic locale; the careful diction and coordinate construction keep everything in this passage on an equal plane: beggars, vendors, and buffalo, none more compelling than another, none exacting more emotional response. Everything seems a subject for Saint-Saens' study, almost scientific in its objectivity, whether noting peculiarities of the local flora or his own sexual proclivities:

> Afternoons he would return to the boathouse or stroll
> on the towpath overhung with yellow mimosas,
> jot botanical notes about date palms and cycads
> or purchase the company of young fauns
> to whom one was invariably kind.

Finally, however, all that he has witnessed and experienced, because of the weight of loss he cannot forget, results in "only a concerto," which serves "as canopic urn / for Luxorian sounds and textures." Art can contain the residue of—but not salvage—a life overburdened with loss.

This complex interplay of the demands of life and of art are explored at greater depth and extent in the O'Keeffe poems. Dooley does not employ a consistent narrative voice through these eleven poems nor even consistent forms, ranging from longer, long-lined poems to prose poems to brief haiku-like gatherings. The point of view is essentially O'Keeffe's, though, as in "Camille in Luxor," emotional distance is often maintained to allow the inherent emotions to emerge from situation and character rather than imposing them with ardent poeticisms and rhetorical clamor. Dooley's approach to narrative stance can be seen clearly in the opening poem of the sequence, "Stieglitz Talking to the Disciples, 1916," in which we hear a longish speech in Stieglitz' voice, contained within quotation marks. Because his voice opens the poem, we do not dwell overmuch on the fact of the quotation marks until Stieglitz' discourse ends, and O'Keeffe's brief comment closes the poem:

I sat

to one side, dressed in black, and did not speak.
My hair came loose and tumbled around my shoulders.

Throughout the sequence, we forget from time to time that these pieces are written, selected, and arranged by someone who never appears in the poems, someone, in fact, who has not overheard but invented the thoughts and voices. Notable, also, is the way O'Keeffe's coda both punctuates and punctures Stieglitz' lofty rhetoric with the physicality of seductiveness.

Such distancing helps moderate the emotional temperature in a situation inherently super-heated: two brilliant, powerful artistic personalities pulled by passion into an adulterous affair and the conflict arising from, among other factors, the disparity in their ages. Dooley deflates some of the potential melodrama by providing behind-the-scenes glimpses when Stieglitz is photographing O'Keeffe. She may be posed, "ready for tragedy," but she can still bristle at his efforts to portray her so:

Don't swear at me if you want me to model.
I could be painting instead, you old goat.
Pose me nude in January—you would.
Like this? Yes—I know the expression.
Quick, take your picture.

("Stieglitz: Early Photographs of O'Keeffe")

Yet these lines also capture, in phrases like "you old goat," the humor and deep affection that underlie the exasperation.

The two prose poems also serve, by virtue of their form, to lend distance to emotionally charged moments. As Dooley argues in an unpublished essay, "The Formalism of the Prose Poem," because prose poems lack meter, line-breaks, and caesurae, the devices for "local emphasis" are fewer, hence the prose poem will "seem more unitary than a poem in verse." Both prose poems in the sequence are set at the Stieglitz family summer home at Lake George, New York, and occur at pivotal moments in the relationship: "Lake George" during O'Keeffe's first visits and "Lake George in Winter" shortly before her departure, alone, to New Mexico. Sandwiched between paragraphs describing her solitary stays, the middle paragraph of "Lake George," with its rush of details, gives a clear sense of tensions already present in the relationship:

> June, and the fields dotted with white daisies. Then relatives arrived, his relatives, with their children who even dared to call her Aunt Georgia, their scampering around and spying where they did not belong, sister-in-law Selma and her ankle-biting bulldog, meals that demanded family disagreements simply to announce one's presence. And his friends couldn't remain in Manhattan or leave behind Cézanne's plastic values and the proper anti-fascist position. Better to climb Prospect Mountain every day and walk through the grove of white birches.

By casting this in prose, Dooley coordinates the details rather than emphasizing some and subordinating others through the structure of verse. Relatives, children, and friends, all with their particular attendant—and intrusive—attitudes, blur into a seasonal distraction. In "Lake George in Winter," a brief novella in its detailing of circumstance, conflicts with Stieglitz over her desire to move West, combined with his deteriorating health, lead O'Keeffe to a solitary retreat. Into this seclusion comes a single visitor, the novelist Jean Toomer. The poem summarizes their simple existence together in an almost cinematic montage:

> He wrote in the mornings and then read to her what he'd written. She liked the tints of his skin, caramel, café au lait, the pink undersides of his hands. She liked his long fingers and the gestures they traced in air. He'd been a Quaker; he spoke once of how the external, the color of skin, was unimportant, unreal. The inner light was what mattered. Only the incorporeal was real.

In scenes that might have been retrieved from the cutting-room floor for *Dr. Zhivago*, we see in long shots their deepening feelings:

> The world seemed exceedingly pure, dazzlingly bright. They drove the Model T onto the surface of the lake and walked on

the wide, glowing expanse till the bitter wind forced them back.
Bits of dark green, ranges of brown, and white, white. Cerulean
sky. Their breath carried their words out onto the wind. When
she grew cold, he took one hand in each of his and rubbed them
against each other. The ice could bear so much weight, them-
selves and the car made no impression. The day was blown glass
of the finest Venetian work. She showed him her favorite birch.

Finally, in "Ghost Ranch," O'Keeffe addresses an imagined Stieglitz on
the roof of her New Mexico home. The tone seems at times petulant, even
accusatory—"If I can climb the ladder at my age, so can you," or "Why
would you never come here, Alfred? / The journey would not have killed
you"—but throughout we sense as well an abiding love and respect, shown,
if nowhere else, in her desire to share her experiences with one she recog-
nizes as soul-mate. In this poem, Dooley captures a painter's way of look-
ing at the world, using grammatical elements to suggest how O'Keeffe
generalizes or particularizes the seen world:

> I never paint flowers any more.
> Flowers wilt. Bone endures. Tulips often die so beautifully,
> I've kept them in bowls while they withered.

Flowers, which perish, notably plural; bone as a collective class of things
which endure. And what do we learn of her character that she keeps cut
flowers to watch the beauty of their passing? She has come to a time in her
life when preserving that which wilts in paint no longer seems a worthy
ambition. Consider as well the use of articles in these lines:

> The first winter I stayed,
> I remember the cows and horses grazing among the cottonwoods,
> the dark mesa to the east, the jagged pink one to the west.

Where many poets would be tempted to generalize by eliminating the
definite articles—"I remember cows and horses grazing among cotton-
woods"—Dooley more accurately presents the way a painter, concerned
with detail, would see the scene: not just "cows and horses" but "*the* cows
and horses," meaning not representatives of a class but these in particular.
He catches as well the abrupt veering from the grand to the mundane evi-
dent in the letters of painters:

> I wish you'd been here when I did the cloud painting.
> Out in the garage, nowhere else would hold it.
> Hurrying to beat the cold. Then I'd climb the red hill
> before sunset and look down at the cool square of sky.
> Milky white. Delicate azure. A kind of glacial light.
> I painted the bottom of the canvas on my knees—
> what if a snake had slipped in? I have to kill them now
> because of the chows. I used to scoop up the rattlers with a shovel
> and pitch them outside the patio.

Artistic vision must accommodate the practicalities of life in the desert. Notice, too, how Dooley uses end-stopped lines to slow the pace; these are not headlong ramblings but considered meditations concerning the course of her life.

The poem concludes with neither giddiness nor cynicism, neither unearned ecstasy nor an equally easy tragic posturing. Instead, she finds herself able to strike a singularly mature balance:

> My dear, I have a curious triumphant feeling about life.
> Seeing it bleak. Knowing it so and walking into it fearless
> because one has no choice. Enjoying one's consciousness.
> You spoiled me for other men, you know.
> How sharply the bonelight winks tonight!
> Far out in the dark are hills which turn angry red
> when a cloud passes. Oh, but in other lights
> they are pink as flesh. What will tomorrow's first colors be?
> Coral? Peach? Pale yellow? Opalescent blue?
> And then the sun will rise.

The assurance that "the sun will rise" may seem slight evidence of triumph, but it indicates an ability to see, at least, past the impending dark. Difficult as Dooley's poetry may be, demanding of us more attention to details of line, syntax, diction, and stance than most current poetry requires or rewards, continued reading may spoil us for other poets.

Allen Hoey

II

A FEW LAST THINGS

He had morning tea with the housekeeper,
a kind, loud woman whose braids
kept coming undone. She talked to him about Jesus;
he said they'd made their peace. She looked unsure.
Why do you want to reach heaven? he teased.
Even if the streets were gold, you'd still want to scrub them.
He'd imagined leaving a testament,
a parchment scroll bearing a secret doctrine
to kindle the initiates, or a plain speech
where "tree" would mean tree and "light" only light,
or words steely with wisdom, polished epigrams
compressing a lifetime's understanding. Wrongheaded again.
He was old, that was all, and sometimes he wrote.
He'd learned to step carefully out to the screen porch.
His wife's African violets still hung from hooks;
he made the housekeeper take care of them.
She said she'd like to get rid of them, those fuzzy leaves
gave her the creeps. Cardinals drank from the birdbaths
his wife insisted he build the year she died.
Birds seemed to fit their world better than humans.
His wife dead, the friend he used to argue philosophy with
dead. He was no longer impressed by the set of meanings
he'd argued for, true enough but small. He needed
to think of his parents so they wouldn't go unremembered,
how they sailed from Poland, seasick every day.
And Natalia, speechless after her stroke,
whose low-pitched laugh he'd fallen in love with.
What good it did for a man, loving a beautiful woman:
his stride quickened, his work flowed, his sense of the world

enlarged, well worth his wife's suffering.
The housekeeper disliked his daughter; she even
mimicked how her mouth was drawn to one side
as she recited a catalogue of mistreatment
and complained of the sons she hadn't brought to see him.
She'd liked laying her dark hair against his arm,
an affectionate child. What he had was
another morning of sunlight and a breeze
stirring the acid-blue hydrangeas. A notebook by the chair
and a pen he could still hold. The revenge by love.

ZORAMEL

The light through the chink in the curtains still woke him
after he'd slept with his best friend's girl.
He'd reach for a cigarette or head for the shower,
keeping the usual routine. Only once
did he start the morning with Scotch—
that, he could tell, was pretty useless.
When he didn't have classes he worked on his novel,
just notes so far about Zoramel, land of high mountains,
where the Piliashtili fled a century ago
when the usurper struck. They were highly evolved,
the Piliashtili, in matters of telepathy,
valuable for those who live on mountains.
He didn't much like her, that was how it started,
the way she was on-again, off-again tore Roland apart.
Why couldn't she see that? She thought dinner was a good idea,
the two who cared most for Roland should get to know each other.
He told her about Zoramel as they walked up the ridge,
how the most sacred ritual was the ceremony of high waters.
The priests kept vigil when the waterfalls started to melt,
and everyone threw dried flowers into the gorge
so that the meadows would bloom again.
She insisted he include something funny in the book,
a forgetful magician or a freckled tomboy who swore.
He picked some chicory for her lapel;
Piliashtili kings dressed in chicory-blue.
The clairvoyant among them lived with the branching of paths,
foreknowledge of possible futures. Glimpses, images,
a banquet held by torchlight, a dungeon. A first-born son

who might share the taint of witch-blood. Not always knowing
when the event would happen or whether the potion drunk,
the quest accepted, fulfilled or annihilated the vision.
They were the ones right for each other, he on top of her,
hands interlocked, he slowly licking her nipples.
Roland was much too old for her. He himself
was now Roland, touching with Roland's fingers,
sensing with Roland's nerves. Her brown eyes and oval face.
The white marks of her bikini straps, she was so small.
They were lovers, she was his destiny! Or they could be
casual lovers, clasping with more laughter than passion:
he gave himself to her, whatever she desired of him.
They had brought this moment into the world and could not
unmake it. Afterward she wept. Since he was the only one there,
his responsibility was to hold her, stroke her hair,
murmur sounds. He was glad she was willing to stay the night,
though she crept to one side of the bed. He still
felt her against him whenever he tried to turn over.
What the book needed was plot. The young prince
could restore the fortunes of the Piliashtili,
that was almost a given, and would probably fall in love.
He hadn't worked out how it would happen. Maybe the villains
could be shape stealers frightened of the sun.
The prince would journey through Zoramel, with or without
a magician. Roland was no help, he didn't like fantasy novels,
and he was obsessed with her, he thought she'd been unfaithful.
He could scarcely teach, let alone work on his thesis.
She hadn't told Roland. But wouldn't she?
Would she be able not to? He found himself telling Roland

about Memnor, Isle of the Glassy Lake, where stood a sacred grove,
and whatsoever was done in that grove, even murder,
was instantly annulled after the deed. The victim
you hacked to pieces stood up and walked out with you.
The prince was under strict instructions not to enter that wood.
The Scotch was making Roland look tearful. If Roland cried,
he would be forced to comfort him.

POLITICS

Campari and soda? You've never tried it?
Why then, my dear, you must. Rather a surprise,
your turning up like this, but a most pleasant one,
I assure you. Why yes, of course I recall last night—
a most agreeable chat—asking you to stop by sometime.
One likes being taken at one's word. What was it
we were talking about? Politics! No wonder I have
such a headache. The topic requires so much Scotch.
Or, in this case, campari. What do you think?
Keep sipping, you may develop a taste for it.
A good drink to order at one of your regular haunts.
Bartenders usually remember, and lovely conversations begin.
Was I carrying on about Reagan? Sometimes I remark how brilliant he was
just to watch people blanch. And we really discussed
my own political career? Speaking of abortions,
which we weren't. I wouldn't call it a sacrifice,
the term sounds rather grand. A conscious decision, certainly.
Who knows if I could have been elected? Family tradition,
connections, inherited wealth, these have been known to help.
And my countenance was thought becoming in those days.
You're much too kind. I was quite a firebrand,
I'd have favored revolution, provided my nearest and dearest
were gunned down first. Mainly the ones who'd put up the money.
I believed blacks in the South should be treated as equals—
this was back when we in the North thought we set an example,
long before your time. Since I was of the right class,
and possessed of a certain wit and charm, it was felt
I could help bring it off. As for foreign affairs,
they're part of a gentleman's education.

But the life wasn't for me, you see. Because the other life was.
The compromise didn't seem all that bad; the fact is
I've always gotten on well with women—I even like
sleeping with them. But not to be able to spend one's vacation on Bali
with a youth slightly underage—not reprehensible there,
I assure you, and nothing to what the late J. Edgar used to do
in his hideaway near San Juan. Those rumors are entirely true.
Perhaps you'll have trouble imagining how repressed we were—
how repressed they were, I can fairly say—though the mighty
found ways of indulging their tastes. A high prelate of the church—
you'd recognize the name—perhaps not, since you were
a Jehovah's Witness—offered to take me along to his favorite
brothel, male, it goes without saying. Out of his robes
and into a suit the vulgarity of which would not have disgraced
a tourist from Dubuque, and off we went. The madam,
male again, cooed like a maitre d' when a film star enters.
The madam was Flatbush Jewish with a lovely Harvard accent. We sat
in red velvet chairs and played cribbage while our churchly Casanova
went off to spread his gospel and partake of the brotherhood of man
with his usual playmate. Black, I believe. Oh no, I merely
chaperone the clergy in bordellos and tell tales afterward.
But as the padre observed when he was once again
clothed in the robes of chastity and goodness, say what I might,
who would believe me? How would a politician react to that?
That's what we expect politicians to do, have opinions and react.
They shouldn't possess too many ideals, but at least a glittering few.
We don't like cynics, rightly, I think, and distrust
too much intelligence. Considering how McNamara and his clever lads
ran the Vietnam War by computer printout, again perhaps rightly.

Would you like to hear my plan for world peace? This would actually work.
Every day after lunch, without fail, every world leader would be
required to masturbate. There'd be no more war. The UN could supervise.
It would have done Margaret Thatcher a world of good, not to mention
the old boys in Beijing. But who listens to reason these days?
One's best ideas go for naught, and the world limps along somehow.
What a very nice idea you had, dropping by, but you look
terribly warm. Perhaps if I simply undo this button.

AND PART OF HER ANUS IN DALLAS

She'd come to a new city, Dallas this time, but all the systems were already in place, everything was connected to everything else. Except that she wasn't, and everyone would expect her to be.

She wrote out her resolutions: Never wear a tux. Never go out with a woman who's wearing a tux. No waitresses, no cashiers, no gym teachers.

The restaurants she went to played songs that were supposed to bring back memories. They didn't. But then she had the memory of hearing those songs in the restaurants.

During Beth and Muriel's party she suddenly got up and said, "I am a woman. I have the right to control my body. I make intelligent choices. I am in charge of my life." Then sat back down.

When you were with someone, that person would always say things and expect you to respond. It was as if they expected a natural ebb and flow, one thing following another, like a play where the actors said their lines and gave each other their cues. But this was real life, wasn't it, no one had written any dialogue.

One of the better paranoid theories was that big business encouraged the breakup of relationships because it doubled the market for basic consumer goods.

Funny how everyone wanted to see patterns. Take the thing with Dan. Muriel asked was she trying to prove something. Mother thought it was her salvation. Karla thought she'd gone crazy. Whereas she and Dan saw it as more of an interlude. It didn't really mean much of anything except that it happened.

Even some of the there's-no-such-thing-as-reality gang probably changed their minds on the downward plunge from the Empire State Building.

She'd open the door and Judy would be shrieking *Do you have any idea what time it is There's no catfood You forgot to buy catfood It's that nurse from the party I saw you looking at her.* Or bayberry candles on the table, chilled wine, dark red roses.

Oh for the days when they drank herbal tea and listened to Phoebe Snow.

Beth and Muriel had been together six years. Amy and Fran had been together four years. Violet and Marie had been together eighteen years. Phyllis and Denise had been together three months.

She turned to the last page: "Her auburn locks blew gently in the warm summer breeze. Brittany had never imagined such happiness was possible. As Chance enfolded her in his strong arms, she knew that the whole future lay open before them."

THE WAITER

For the last time he put on the frilled white shirt,
the black pants, tied on the apron with deep pockets.
He gathered the slick white menus and greeted
the early arrivals. He smiled the accustomed smile
as he took the drink orders, suggested the blackened redfish
and ground fresh pepper on the Boston lettuce.
An older couple exclaimed at the scalloped butter rosettes.
In the past he had made up stories about the people he served,
the young husband who wouldn't look at his wife,
afraid to reveal so much love; the woman who ate alone
reading Agatha Christie. He had learned
to maintain a proper retreat; that was more loving.
All he wanted tonight was to freshen the iced teas,
to talk about bread pudding and Kahlua cheesecake.
When he moved his lumbering frame back to the kitchen,
placing the orders for chicken with artichoke hearts,
none of the others lingered to speak, Bill with another story
about the new baby, or Ron, not high tonight, who'd said
he looked like a big teddy bear and put his hands on him.
Just as well get used to the discomfort others would feel,
how the monk's robe would mean he was not the same,
himself not a body like other bodies, the self withering in prayer.
As in work. The woman in the green dress had changed her mind
and wanted dessert. Certainly. More of his tables filling up,
tonight would be hectic. Then sometime after eleven
he would pull the door shut behind him, perhaps with
no more than the usual goodbyes, and begin his journey
to a room with white walls and a hard bed
where he could be nothing and God could be always.

DIRT

You think your place is a mess? You should have
seen Frankie's. I never told you about Frankie?
We go back a long way. He was the only one who didn't
think it was weird for a Texan to chew bouillon cubes
or read Camus on the school bus. We argued a lot
about Angst and what kind of car we'd buy
if we had five hundred bucks. Frankie,
this is typical, wanted a Chevy Vega even though
I told him the aluminum around the engine fell apart
after ten thousand miles. We were at this car lot, see,
and straight as a shot Frankie heads for a Vega
whose insides are completely burned out.
It figured, it really did. And dirt:
he had a system about dirt. Wait long enough
and someone else will clean it for you.
Usually me—you noticed I'm kind of compulsive?
Once, this was one of the times he was in college,
what did I find by his mattress but a rubber
in a coffee cup. Used. Oh, but things were worse
after he got married the second time. She was pregnant
by someone else and, this is hard to believe, messier than Frankie.
I've seen everything mixed up in stacks on the floor,
steak knives, bills, dirty diapers, dog food,
the library was on his ass about Kierkegaard,
and from the street you could see the grow lights
for his marijuana plants, even though the cops
had busted him twice. Frankie had a good heart, though,
he put up with me all these years, and he took in this old dog
who'd been hit by a car. One afternoon, he may have had
his sociology degree by then, I go over to his place.

The door's open, and Frankie's asleep, blanket
pulled up to his chin except for his long bushy beard,
and sticking up from under the bed, he has a bed by then,
are the stiff legs of that poor old dog. I shake him:
"Frankie, Frankie, the dog's dead." "He's just sleeping."
"Frankie. The dog is *dead*." He went right back to sleep.
Then there were the times we smoked dope
when Frankie would say he couldn't understand
why there was so much evil, since the whole world
was only inside his head—a scary idea. We lost touch
when I started teaching, he said I'd sold out.
Then a couple of years ago I heard he was working
in a bank. Then I heard he was delivering pizzas.
I was dating an ex-girlfriend of his, real pretty,
not as pretty as you—oh yes, you like it—and we thought about
ordering a pizza. When Frankie arrived we'd be standing there
stark naked. But we never did.

CAMILLE IN LUXOR:
SAINT-SAENS VISITS EGYPT, 1896

To be wakened by the croaking of frogs and peepers
in the blinding dawn—an Egyptian winter
remote from Parisian fogs, air so dry
the dust fell easily off. By noon,
white heat glowed on the river
flowing like liquid tin, and the dahabeeyahs
floated without a ripple.
Mornings he was content to observe
the half-hidden temple rising above the quay,
or look across the river to villages built of mud, where
buffaloes sank up to the shoulder dragging their yokes,
or in the marketplace to be jostled by guides,
beggars, donkey boys, Copts tattooed with crosses,
a one-eyed vendor hawking morsels of roast mutton.
Cacophonies of language, such strange perfumes.
Afternoons he would return to the houseboat or stroll
on the towpath overhung with yellow mimosas,
jot botanical notes about date palms and cycads
or purchase the company of young fauns
to whom one was invariably kind.
And the nights! Silver light and gray shadows,
as if they were days under a spell of enchantment
when the moon rose over the hills and lit the Nile
like a softer sun. The Nubian boatmen
sang strophes of love unfulfilled,
and his telescope found stars tinged greenish and red.
He joined nocturnal excursions to Karnak
riding down long avenues of stone rams,
an Academician of sixty on a donkey,

anxious to raise his lamp to examine the wall-paintings,
profiles of gods half-bestial, histories
reduced to inscriptions and colored emblems,
then sealed in such disproportioned tombeaus.
The explorers returned to a feast by the river,
a sheep roasted whole, drums and reed flute,
dancing females, the dragoman chanting Arabic poems,
far from the Paris to which he must return,
where a young wife could neglect her duty
and a son fall dead from a window,
return with only a concerto as canopic urn
for Luxorian sounds and textures—the flapping of sails,
Ali grunting, a crocodile moving in the moonlit water—
even the thud of the propellers as the steamer
carried the voyager toward home,
which no longer existed.

SWEET YOUTH

Young enough to be my son? For the first time, yes.
Too skinny and too short and wearing an earring.
"I've never slept with anyone less than ten years older,"
he explained in the Thai restaurant as he wolfed down
heavily-gingered beef and gulped glasses of water.
He introduced the proprietor, Madame Dang,
and told me he'd majored in religion. "Nothing practical.
Cool, maybe. Post-modern, even. But practical, never.
Last year I blackened my face with shoe polish
and went to a Halloween party as Butterfly McQueen.
You don't look amused. Well, get over it. I still carry
my ex-lover's picture in my wallet at all times.
I never dreamed it was possible to hurt so much."
Mother died this August. I saw her afterward
in the Pittsburgh airport, three different women,
each with a red coat, thinning salt-and-pepper hair,
one even with a limp. In the hospital
she lay comatose on her side, tubes in her nose.
When I told her I loved her, she gasped even more harshly,
turned over on her back, then breathed as before
two more hours. As a friend expressed it, with mother
and father dead, there's no one left between you
and the edge of the world.
"Can you believe this music? 'And sometimes when we touch,
the honesty's too much.' Boo. Yuck. Yech.
'The sodomy's too much'—now that's more like it.
I should give Madame Dang a tape of some good Europop.
Europop is something like technopop. You've heard of
the Talking Heads? If not, we have no future.

Don't you drink anything stronger than jasmine tea?
An experienced pharmaceutical connoisseur,
such as myself, can help you ease your sorrow.
Just put yourself in these loving hands."

A LITTLE HUNGER

Not the puffy beef tacos, her absolute favorites,
though the Iranian owner attempted to make them
as fat-free as possible. No refried beans ever ever
so chalupas were out. Chicken fajitas? They could
order chicken fajitas for two and she could let Eric
eat more than half. They could get corn tortillas
but Eric really preferred flour, well so did she
for that matter, and he liked beef better than chicken,
so maybe the combo fajitas for two and she could coax him
to eat some of the chicken. She'd limit herself on
chips and salsa and leave most of the guacamole (so good!
and so fattening!) and all of the sour cream (she could be
strong) for Eric. He'd suggested Mexican tonight because
he knew how much she loved it. He liked pleasing her
and wanted her to be pleased. He was close, he was closer
than anyone ever had been, to proposing, and if—
she wasn't going beyond if—he did, he'd expect her to say yes.
She would say yes. She'd given little hints she would,
like when Barbara and Raul got engaged and she said
what a neat couple they made because they were such friends
and had so much fun together, which was what she and Eric
said about themselves. She hadn't wanted to marry anyone
before law school and in law school who had time
to do anything but order in pizza and read cases? Mushrooms
and pepperoni with extra cheese. Yum. At work
she could exist on microwave popcorn (unsalted,
unbuttered, as much as she wanted) and diet Pepsi.
Eric said he loved her figure, which was sweet, but
did anyone really love cellulite thighs? After marriage

you had to expect some weight gain (from Eric, too,
who was a chicken-fried steak kind of guy, she'd cook it
and have to eat her share of it) and after a child
still more pounds but everyone expected you to diet then.
Damn, there was no way out of a margarita (as if she
needed liquor to say yes) but she could gracefully
stop at one. She'd eaten entirely too many chips
and Eric was prone to ordering chocolate desserts
she at least had to taste. If he spent the night,
and he probably would, she had his favorite
cream-filled doughnuts for breakfast, and with coffee and juice
she could get away with taking only part of a doughnut.
A little bite. Leaving him almost all of the filling.

LILLIAN'S ELEGY

No thanks, I have these Kleenex, and besides
I'm all cried out for a while. Daddy and I
went out to the grave this morning
before it got too hot. Some of the stands had fallen,
but the wreaths were still pretty. So many roses. Gladiolas.
Daddy tired himself out picking up the stands,
he's lying down now, and you know what he said?
He said to me, "Mother, why can't I be the one
lying there instead of Paul?" Of course I feel the same,
but you know how he doesn't talk much,
it almost broke my heart all over again.
He's fond of you, but has he ever said so?
You'd think there'd be a sense of relief,
Paul was sick for so long, but where is it?
Do you feel any? I don't feel any.
He looked so thin in the coffin, but natural,
I told Mr. Anders, Mr. Hubert Anders, the old one,
what a good job they'd done, considering.
He was small when he was born, not even six pounds.
But healthy. I counted fingers and toes
when they brought him to me. Not that I couldn't
have loved a nine-toed baby as well as any woman.
Sometimes we'd bathe him in the sink while we ate,
he was happy playing as long as he could see us. Never once
climbed out of his crib the way Betty did.
You couldn't keep that child in a playpen
no matter how many squeeze toys you threw in.
Such a fine little fellow in his new jeans
when he waved goodbye and caught the school bus.

Some of the children were cruel right from the start.
And in high school, or earlier, junior high,
they'd call him—ugly names—when he walked down the hall.
Not that he told me. You may not know
what a parent goes through, managing to keep still.
Did he ever tell you about his girlfriend,
yes he had one, an albino, poor homely thing,
had a nervous breakdown their junior year.
Oh, she's married and divorced and has a baby,
just like everyone else. Now I'm going to laugh,
I don't want to, but Paul wouldn't mind,
we laughed about this only last month.
He was thirteen, and his voice teacher,
thank goodness, wouldn't let him sing
"I'm Gonna Wash That Man Right out of My Hair."
The night of his high school graduation
I said to him, "You think you're gay, don't you?
Well, you're not." Because he might not have been,
and he might have met a nice girl in college,
and he was just as good as any of those others.
"Oh yes I am," he said right back. You've seen him
when he was like that. Paul could be definite.
Very definite. From then on I worried even more.
Because what could I tell him? And for me not to be able
to give advice, well, Paul would swear that never happened,
and you might too. The first friend Paul brought to meet us
was eleven months to the day younger than me. I bit my tongue
to keep from asking where he bought his toupee.
At least Paul did better later, first Michael

and then you. I wonder that Michael wasn't at the funeral,
you don't suppose, no, I'm too tired to suppose.
To tired to do much except go lie down beside Daddy.
The thought of that bed. Right before daylight,
to see Paul's face come I-spying up over the crib.
"Ooh," he'd say. "Ooh." I'd change and powder him
and tuck him up against Daddy, then go down to warm the milk.
Betty never woke up. Slept as hard as she did everything else.
If she doesn't go home tomorrow, we may get into
a knockdown drag-out fight complete with hair pulling.
When I'd get back to our room, Paul's fist
would be wrapped around Daddy's little finger,
and the two of them would be talking. Sometimes
I was convinced I could follow what they were saying.
I'd prop up the pillows in the rocking chair, then
one of us would feed him and the other would burp him.
Things were different then. That was life.

SUN PICTURES

Suppose we tried to recapture in photographs
our morning drive to Rochester. One year ago today.
I'd want to take pictures of the towns' names,
homage to the classical world whose virtues
would flourish again: Ithaca, so that a wanderer
will build his last dwelling by tranquil water;
Romulus, so that the wild hills will nourish
a founder of cities; Ovid, so that the native tongue
will acquire potency and wit. We'd choose
exempla of the truest American pastoral,
hundred-year oaks, brick houses with plain Doric columns,
white clapboard churches. We'd add details simply because
we liked them: the plaque for the Philomathic Library,
cornfields with signs indicating the breed:
Garst 8808. I would charge these cultivated hills
with longing, a Tennesseean's nostalgia
for green after green. We'd need shots of ourselves
as you drove through the August morning,
Cayuga Lake off to our right. You'd brought
red seedless grapes and bottles of sparkling water,
lime-flavored, passionfruit-flavored.
We said little except to confirm our sense
that at every curve the road presented significant objects,
so that the act of seeing became the act of vision.
At last our two-lane reached the highway,
reminding us we had a destination:
not illumination, but history. Your house:
kitchen of light-grained wood, dining room
hung with prints of Shakespearean actors.

You showed me the museum membership cards,
I could use your husband's. But lunch before art.
The Art Deco diner—you knew I'd love it—waitresses
capped and aproned in black and white, framed clippings
(Titanic Sinks; We Like Ike for Four More Years),
photos of stars: Bacall, Louise Brooks, Montgomery Clift.
You told me when Eastman, old and sick, killed himself,
he left a note: "Why should I wait? My work is done."
Today at noon in the Alamo Gardens, while tourists
snap pictures of each other, I remember how we
hurried under the porte-cochere, showed our cards,
ascended a hardwood staircase to the rooms where Eastman
slept and thought, turned into a brief history
of the art his genius kept giving means to.
You showed me a sepia photograph of the Louvre, off-center angle,
textures of stone, only twenty years into the art.
The sheen on the Weston pepper. "Erotic." "Funny."
Steichen's Duse, how her long neck seemed somehow
the key to tragedy. "And the fuzzy focus. Tragedy
depends on a slight blur." Muybridge, who murdered
his wife's lover, created an atlas of motion,
naked beings as noble as ancient gods.
And his Yosemite, sheer walls fringed daintily with trees,
rocks like buttresses, spires, domes, skulls, viscera.
Your favorite was Julia Margaret Cameron:
her husband sits in majesty as if from another sphere,
white hair gleaming like sea foam, hands touching
a golden chain—"O what good it does to one's soul
to go forth!" she wrote. She would have made you

one of her beautiful puritans, hair parted and coiled,
drapery pulled about to conceal your shape
so that you emerge dramatically from darkness,
a form for inwardness. She began at fifty. Fifty years
to prepare for art. The Larry Clark kept drawing me back:
scrawled across the top in capital letters,
DEATH IS MORE PERFECT THAN LIFE. His creed, the hometown
James Dean who perches on the bed with a revolver,
bare chest, slicked-back dark hair? The distance he keeps
invites the partners who'll never reach him, wildness
pressed in, as if neither body nor soul could offer
y to his x, the globe itself is inadequate.
Even death is inadequate. A card tells us
he overdosed on heroin shortly thereafter.
Or do the words provide only texture, played off against
the shape the human object takes, the image
held up against the words, the words leading back to the image?
Today by the Alamo the trees each carry a nameplate:
pecan; mescal bean. A bed of geraniums re-creates
the Lone Star flag. A gray-haired woman about sixty
hands me her Polaroid and asks if I'll take a picture.
Second honeymoon, she winks, indicating her husband,
golfing cap, walrus mustache, pale blue guayabera,
who obligingly grins. They pose stiff in front of the wall,
a sweep of oak branch behind them. "One more," she calls,
leaning against his shoulder. Already the first shot's
nearly dried into form. At Eastman House
we stopped in front of Verdi, the young Oscar Wilde,
attempting to read one expression for a final disclosure.

Freeze-frame: transfixed by the Cartier-Bresson:
I kept glancing at you. He bicycles into the sun-blur,
the French boy, passing a flight of stairs. Chance
plus vigilance plus camera equals art, I teased.
You touched my sleeve. Not chance. All elements,
you said, were pre-arranged. We'd come to the end
of our tour. These are the sun pictures I printed:
descent of the stairs. Red-gold hair.
Unadorned white linen. In the midday glare
wife and husband reclaim their camera, bid me
goodbye and walk off. I vanish from their lives.

II

O'KEEFFE
AND
STIEGLITZ

"An American art, that is what I ask of you,
an art worthy of this land, do I not have the right to ask it?
Paint your pictures and I will hang them,
I will find buyers, but they must be truly your pictures,
shall a young painter be content to mimic the Europeans?
When you have this vast continent, unexplored,
unexplored in the figurative sense, my meaning was quite clear,
the American landscape, these enormous buildings, must you
kiss a raddled whore in Montmartre to imagine yourself a painter?
But of course you're right to admire Braque and Duchamp and Kandinsky,
what do you mean, not Kandinsky, he puts emotions on canvas,
that remark was crude and uncalled for, young man,
you want to paint greatly yet you lack civilization,
think of a man like Goethe, no American can compare with him,
indeed I am not contradicting myself, never
I emphasize never do I contradict myself, but if you
cannot follow the turns of thought in civilized discourse—
Goethe I say Goethe had the romantic heart, the romantic soul
but an intellect sharp as the scientist's lens,
how dare you say, 'Oh yes, but I am from New Jersey,'
was Weimar Weimar before Goethe made it so?
You must make of New Jersey a second Weimar,
if it is necessary to your genius you will do it, a stoa of
philosophers and artists, yourself a Goethe who goes on creating,
or learn a lesson from Ibsen, the master builder himself,
he could have stopped, he would still have been great,
but he kept quarrying and quarrying out of himself,
you speak of baring your soul in paint, is your soul
really that small, can a few paltry canvases, I am not

calling your canvases paltry, contain all of a human soul,
an Ibsen throws out soul here, soul there, and always there is more,
no matter how old or weary he goes on, no no I agree,
John Gabriel Borkman is no *Hedda, Hedda* we can never forget,
but he goes on, forcing himself to climb his towers and mountains,
When We Dead Awaken, and when shall we who are not dead awaken,
when shall you who are young awaken?" I sat
to one side, dressed in black, and did not speak.
My hair came loose and tumbled around my shoulders.

STIEGLITZ: EARLY PHOTOGRAPHS OF O'KEEFFE

The fingers, poised around buttons of bone.
Eyes of an herb woman in a Chinese village.
Luxurious hair wrapped up around her head;
breasts as white and innocent as her arms.
Light glowing on white flanks.
The shadowy pubis.

> Champagne, M'sieu? A poor girl like me
> isn't used to such delicacies.
> How do I look in your derby hat?
> If I let the shirt fall open,
> surely no one would object. I think
> I would now like a little champagne.
> Oh, M'sieu. M'sieu is much too kind.

In a white gown of many folds the woman stands,
her hair dark and flowing. She is ready for tragedy
and will answer to the name Andromache.
Andromache owns the fury of Clytemnestra
but will not express it. By this she comprehends
nobility. Her eyes see her child torn from her grasp
and smashed to the rocks below. The loss of a husband
is every woman's lot. You will not hear
the howls of her lamentations.

> Here in front of a painting, my love,
> I will pose you. Only a corner of the painting.
> They will see this woman is an artist,
> her work stretches out of our sight

but we will follow. Can't you hold still, damn it,
another plate ruined. Hold still while I make you immortal.
This is how woman looks when she creates.
No, love, I am wrong, it is you who make me immortal,
you who restore art to one whom art had renounced.
To photograph one person over many years,
the whole become one photograph of love.

Don't swear at me if you want me to model.
I could be painting instead, you old goat.
Pose me nude in January—you would.
Like this? Yes, I know the expression.
Quick, take your picture.
You can photograph me for a lifetime
and never comprehend the mystery.
But every woman should have a lover like you.
I am yours. Enter! Enter!

Spring: usually chilly. Lilacs opened heart-shaped leaves among the pine and white birch. Grape shoots were velvety pink. She liked to wade in the streams, hunting for cresses.

June, and the fields dotted with white daisies. Then relatives arrived, his relatives, with their children who even dared to call her Aunt Georgia, their scampering around and spying where they did not belong, sister-in-law Selma and her ankle-biting bulldog, meals that demanded family disagreements simply to announce one's presence. And his friends couldn't remain in Manhattan or leave behind Cézanne's plastic values and the proper anti-fascist position. Better to climb Prospect Mountain every day and walk through the grove of white birches.

Autumn was best for painting. Cicadas screeched in the evenings and Canada geese flew over the lake. Hillsides of sugar maples turned red. At sunrise the trunk of an old birch was bleached white, but the leaves were radiant gold. By November the sky darkened; heavy clouds drizzled. She was exhausted and pale, painted out, they had to return to the city. The mountain turned brownish-purple except for patches of evergreen.

JUDITH

She presided over the dining room,
Miss Marblehead, from a fringed scarf
atop the china closet, granting us
the favor of her royal simper
and a breast absent-mindedly exposed.
Heroine of the Hebrews indeed! As if to save her people
she only needed antimacassars for the horsehair sofa.
We dug the hole deep that night.
How the spade resounded in the hard earth,
the sweat cooled quickly on our bodies.
All three conspirators raised her high,
then let her drop.
That's earth smearing your face, milady.
Let the relatives wail at her absence—
one of their forebears had, after all, purchased her—
feigning ignorance was quite agreeable.
I could have but did not explain:
artists make the best critics.

A CONVERSATION

No, it would be quite impossible,
we are agreed. Hush, my dear,
you need not argue. Our views are identical.
You do not feel the physical craving,
I would not expect you to.
You can see, even more clearly than I,
the practical side, how our life, our two lives,
would fracture, inevitably diminished
by increase. Think of the hours I spend
preparing the canvas, mixing each color with a separate brush.
What infant would respect those hours?
Or even the days I spend without paint,
walking by Lake George when lilacs begin to open,
or simply waiting. Cooking. Yes, I would be diverted.
The poem you wrote for me, about the woman who carries
dawn in her womb. How does that feel, I wonder?
No, I do not know. How free, and how wise,
you are, not imagining you need a son
or another daughter. No daughter of ours
would turn away from the light, from her little son,
like your poor girl, or would a child we made
be smothered by us, by a surfeit of life, or art,
which seem to be the same thing. Your photographs
will carry you forward. That is enough.
For me—swirls of azure on stark white?
A shape. That's all, merely a shape. A flower,
oh, a black iris. We will not speak of sacrifice.
Let us end this long conversation. Come to bed.

FLOWERS

1

larger than the humans who stand in front of them

2

like butterflies pinned open
or lit from within

3

fringed orchid
exploding with light at the center

4

the hollyhock's black sheen glows with red,
and the larkspur, blue crystals of larkspur!

5

the white trumpet-flower
all its curves are hard-edged

6

the shape at the top of the bleeding heart
an apple dipped in ashes

7

a ribbon of light
through the green corn

dark leaves, light veins
reaching in opposing directions

morning by morning
a drop of dew slips down the veins
to pool in the sheath's dark center

8

if you think the stamens and pistils are phallic
the lip-shaped petals a vulva
I don't

9

they're cheaper than models
and they don't move

10

the large white flower with the golden heart
is something I have to say about white

11

petals of the white rose unfold
like a drama at Epidaurus

12

the dark spider at the heart of the scarlet poppy

13

purple iris
tonguelike, velvety, purplish-gray petals
uncurling into blackness

14

when the painter is unafraid
the result is calmness

15

stripes of the jack-in-the-pulpit
this time the interior all black
a thin stalk of white rises from the plump candle

the final variation the most abstract
only the jack
against a doorway of white

OBSERVATIONS

1. What can you say to a young painter? Go home and work.

2. Once I was a little girl wondering how to paint moonlight on snow.

3. Sometimes it takes courage to paint a flower.

4. I can't understand people who want something and don't grab for it.

5. A house should be just a shelter. I've sometimes wished for a fire to rid me of possessions. A shell, a stone, a skull—these are enough for decoration.

6. Work is the most interesting thing one knows to do.

7. Why paint something if you don't love it?

STIEGLITZ AGING

The man explained to her—he could not stop explaining—
that a true artist like herself didn't have to travel.
I have all the world around me, he would say,
gesturing. Your thin clear air, your New Mexico highlands
would finish my heart. The handkerchief
fluttered around his mouth to ward off germs.
The woman didn't want to believe that categories
like "still vital wife" and "aging husband" applied to them.
She had married a man of wisdom and force and genius.
Chilly days, he wore cape, herringbone coat, sweater
over shirt and tie, woolen underwear, porkpie hat
indoors. He was still a devil with the women,
at least she wondered, he photographed dear little Dorothy
nude in the meadow, vapid as a nymph by Boucher,
though thus far no guilty embrace interrupted,
no lipstick in the bathroom, no whiskers smelling of woman.
When his wife thought of the west, he knew and was afraid.
She arranged the elegant horse skull, desert-white,
and began to paint. Out there, each day arrived clear,
like the ring of a hammer striking something hard.
He liked to say to others when she was present,
there has been one who stood by me, this girl from Texas.
He spoke as if he had not learned that one who accepts disciples
invites abandonment. History was not on his side, the departing ones
told him, his holy of holies, the artist's fulfillment,
outdated and, worse, bourgeois. Her only solution
was to let the canvases of bone take shape.
She stuck a fabric flower in the empty eye socket.

The two of them held hands and listened to Beethoven.
He photographed her nude, as he had at first,
her buttocks like sacred objects, heart-shaped,
inviting the touch. From her vantage point on the mesa
the sky would be ripped by half a dozen thunderstorms at once.

They'd never wintered there. Now she was alone at the lake with only a housekeeper. She couldn't paint. Didn't want to. She couldn't bear even the thought of Alfred. New York was unthinkable.

She did have one visitor. Jean, Jean Toomer, drove up from New York to see her. She didn't mind him, he knew how to be quiet. When she opened the door and saw the look on his face, she whispered, "I've been ill, I've been ill," and fell in his arms.

They existed together quite simply. He wrote in the mornings and then read to her what he'd written. She liked the tints of his skin, caramel, café au lait, the pink undersides of his hands. He'd been a Quaker; he spoke once how the external, the color of skin, was unimportant, unreal. The inner light was what mattered. Only the incorporeal was real.

Deep snow drifted around the farmhouse. The world seemed exceedingly pure, dazzlingly bright. They drove the Model T onto the surface of the ice and walked on the wide, glowing expanse till the bitter wind forced them back. Bits of dark green, ranges of brown, and white, white. Cerulean sky. Their breath carried their words out onto the wind. When she grew cold, he took one hand in each of his and rubbed them against each other. The ice could bear so much weight, themselves and the car made no impression. The day was blown glass of finest Venetian work. She showed him her favorite birch.

In the evenings they sat by the fire. She talked, for once, about painting. Realism and abstraction were the same. The purest form of realism led to abstraction. And mere shape, a painter's envisioning of forms, pointed back toward something real. He took her hand. Both of them played with the kittens. The white kitten liked laps, her dress buttons, and his sheaf of manuscript. The firelight falling on Jean. The syllable "Jean" becoming a potent spell.

Oh, he must leave. She knew that, they both knew it. She had never imagined this crossroads. He would leave when she said the word. Tomorrow they would walk on the ice again.

After he left, she wrote him every day. I want you, she wrote. Sometimes terribly. But I like it that I am quite apart from you like the snow on the mountain. She did not know if she meant it.

NEW MEXICO

1

at first the hills look small

2

no rain
so the flowers didn't come

3

souvenir of the first summer
a barrel of bones

4

gray hills
all the same color and shape
a hot-colored brown hill

5

the long dark lines of the Pedernal
sky a pale greenish blue
high up, a white moon

6

the coolness and sweetness of evening
fragrance of the poison jimson weed

7

against the gray mountains
someone had imposed a cross

it was large enough to crucify a man

8

I heard the Penitente songs
and painted the dark crosses

9

the black rocks
have lain a long time
with sun and wind and blowing sand

10

keeping the fire burning
to warm where we intended to sleep

I stood on a rug and wore gloves to paint

reading *Taras Bulba* aloud
hills and stars overhead

11

gray sage, gray wet sand underfoot
gray hills, pale moon
the wind blew the coffee out of our cups

12

paintings grow by pieces
from what is around

13

low mountains covered with trees
a bare spot near the top
the shape of a leaping deer

14

painting pelvis bones
the blue from holding them against the sky

15

footmarks
around the dead cedar
he must have been dancing

GHOST RANCH

Come up to the roof! I would say.
If I can climb the ladder at my age, so can you.
Perfectly mad-looking country, isn't it,
hills and cliffs and washes thrown up by God
and left to tumble where they will.
Before the light fades, look at those gouged cliffs to the north—
a giant's sandcastle with saw-toothed turrets and spires.
Reddish rock at the bottom, then golden
solidified sand dunes, and the top's
gray fossil-filled gypsum and limestone.
See how the light hits the mountains from both front and back,
the distances appear in layers. I love to see my bare hills
glowing like red-hot coals before the abrupt dark.
With luck there'll be a thunderstorm tonight.
Our summer cloudbursts sweep in waterfalls over the rock face
and tumble down the arroyos. Sit down in that chair, I'd say,
I've brought blankets and a lantern and a pitcher of iced fruit juice.
Tell your friends in New York you spent an evening
on the roof of Ghost Ranch looking at the sky.
Rancho de los Brujos, the Spaniards called it,
which means witches, not ghosts. I've seen neither.
Come up here around Easter, though, and you'll hear the Penitentes.
They drag their crosses and cart of death
to an unmarked chapel quite nearby.
I hear their chant, all night their one song of grief,
the high notes of a homemade flute,
the dull thuds of their cactus whips.
Their acts seem natural in a land with more sky than earth.
I never paint flowers any more.

Flowers wilt. Bone endures. Tulips often die so beautifully,
I've kept them in bowls while they withered.
A fine moon tonight, large and lopsided,
tinges of rose and almost orange.
Why would you never come here, Alfred?
The journey would not have killed you.
The clouds over Lake George are nothing to these.
In November, chamiso bushes by the road turn golden,
and the wild asters bloom. The first winter I stayed,
I remember the cows and horses grazing among the cottonwoods,
the dark mesa to the east, the jagged pink one to the west.
The very first time I came looking for Ghost Ranch,
these were the directions: follow the road northwest from Espanola,
turn where you see an animal skull.
I loved the stunted piñons, the junipers and cedars.
I'd bathe in the narrow irrigation ditches.
So many different earth colors,
brown, orange, soft green, Naples yellow, even violet.
I wanted to paint with the hues of this land,
but the ocher soil was too sandy for pigment.
You aged so needlessly, Alfred. Pointlessly!
But our marriage was really very good.
You enjoyed gloom, but I could make you laugh.
I could put up with nonsense from a man
obsessed by truth. After your stroke,
when I left to come back here, you understood.
How could I paint if I stayed to hold your hand?
You told me once that true marriage is tragic;
it leads two people apart.

But we were keenly interested in each other's work.
I wish you'd been here when I did the cloud painting.
Out in the garage, nowhere else would hold it.
Hurrying to beat the cold. Then I'd climb the red hill
before sunset and look down at the cool square of sky.
Milky white. Delicate azure. A kind of glacial light.
I painted the bottom of the canvas on my knees—
what if a snake had slipped in? I have to kill them now
because of the chows. I used to scoop up the rattlers with a shovel
and pitch them outside the patio. Such elegant dogs,
their fluffy plumes, their little coyote trots.
Visitors must be careful. Their teeth are sharp.
I've seen more than one pair of shoes fill with blood.
My dear, I have a curious triumphant feeling about life.
Seeing it bleak. Knowing it so and walking into it fearless
because one has no choice. Enjoying one's consciousness.
You spoiled me for other men, you know.
How sharply the bonelight winks tonight!
Far out in the dark are hills which turn angry red
when a cloud passes. Oh, but in other lights
they are pink as flesh. What will tomorrow's first colors be?
Coral? Peach? Pale yellow? Opalescent blue?
And then the sun will rise.

"Camille in Luxor: Saint-Saens Visits Egypt, 1896": Camille Saint-Saens wrote his fifth piano concerto, the "Egyptian," in 1896 following a winter in Luxor. Saint-Saens blamed his wife, who was much younger than he, for the death of their oldest son and broke off the marriage.

"Sun Pictures": "Sun pictures" was an early name for photographs. Eadweard Muybridge is well-known for his pioneering studies of bodies in motion. Julia Margaret Cameron is one of the most famous Victorian photographers.

O'Keeffe and Stieglitz

Sources for Part II include biographies of Georgia O'Keeffe by Laurie Lisle and Jan Castro; *Georgia O'Keeffe* (Viking Press, 1976), a volume of reproductions of O'Keeffe's work; and Stieglitz's photographs of O'Keeffe, reproduced in *Georgia O'Keeffe* (Metropolitan Museum of Art, no date). Some of the poems make use of O'Keeffe's own words, directly or adapted.

Alfred Stieglitz (1864-1946) was not only a pioneering photographer, but also a magazine editor and gallery owner who promoted the work of many talented artists. He immediately recognized the great ability of Georgia O'Keeffe (1887-1986). Stieglitz was separated from his wife; they had one daughter, who suffered a mental breakdown after the birth of a child ("A Conversation"). Stieglitz and O'Keeffe became lovers and married after Stieglitz and his wife divorced.

"Stieglitz Talking to the Disciples, 1916": *John Gabriel Borkman* and *When We Dead Awaken* are late plays by Ibsen.

"Lake George": The Stieglitz family had a summer home on Lake George in upstate New York.

"Judith": The bust of Judith which O'Keeffe found offensive as inferior art was in the Stieglitz family home on Lake George. Judith saved the Israelites by slaying Holofernes.

David Dooley works as a legal assistant in San Antonio, Texas. He has received degrees in English from Johns Hopkins University and the University of Tennessee. His first book of poems, *The Volcano Inside* (Story Line Press, 1988), earned the Nicholas Roerich Poetry Prize. Mr. Dooley's poetry and criticism has appeared in numerous magazines, including *The Hudson Review* and the *Beloit Poetry Journal*.